MW00805242

YOU CAN BE A WOMAN™ MOVIE MAKER

Mary McLaglen

Maureen Gosling

Paula Weinstein

Judith Love Cohen

Editing:
Lee Rathbone

Cascade Pass, Inc.
www.cascadepass.com

Published by Cascade Pass, Inc., Suite C-105
4223 Glencoe Avenue
Marina del Rey, CA 90292-8801
Phone (310) 305-0210
Printed in Hong Kong by South China Printing Co. Ltd.

First Edition 2003
You Can Be a Woman Movie Maker was written by Mary McLaglen, Maureen Gosling, Paula Weinstein and Judith Love Cohen, Art Direction by David Katz, and edited by Lee Rathbone. Graphics design by Kana Tatakawa of Momo Communications, Inc.

This book is one of a series that emphasizes the value of art and other non-traditional careers by depicting real women whose careers provide inspirational role models.

Other books in the series include:
You Can Be A Woman Architect
You Can Be A Woman Paleontologist
You Can Be A Woman Zoologist
You Can Be A Woman Soccer Player
You Can Be A Woman Meteorologist
You Can Be A Woman Egyptologist
You Can Be A Woman Entomologist
You Can Be A Woman Botanist
You Can Be A Woman Marine Biologist
You Can Be A Woman Softball Player

Library of Congress Cataloging-in-Publication Data
McLaglen, Mary, 1959-
You can be a woman movie maker / Mary McLaglen, Paula Weinstein, Maureen Gosling. – 1st ed.
p. cm.
Summary: Describes what a career in film production and direction is like, using examples from the life of Mary McLaglen, a Line Producer for motion pictures.
ISBN 1-880599-63-5 (Paper & DVD); 1-880599-64-3 (Hard Cover & DVD)
1. Motion pictures – Production and direction – Juvenile literature. 2. Motion pictures – Production and direction – Vocational guidance – Juvenile literature. 3. Women motion picture producers and directors – United States – Biography – Juvenile Literature. [1. Motion pictures – Production and direction – Vocational guidance. 2. Motion picture producers and directors. 3. McLaglen, Mary 1959- 4. Women – Biography. 5. Vocational guidance.] I. Weinstein, Paula. II. Gosling, Maureen. III. Title.
PN1995.9.P7M38 2003 2003008156
791.43'0232'023–dc21

Dedication

This book is dedicated by author Mary McLaglen to her father, Andrew McLaglen who has inspired Mary, from a young age, to reach for the stars.

This book is dedicated by author Maureen Gosling to her niece, Emily Gosling Ludwig and her nephew Alex Gosling Ludwig: “May your dreams never be burdens.”

This book is dedicated by author Paula Weinstein to her daughter, Hannah, so that she will always follow her dreams.

Hot Springs, VA, is a beautiful town. Off the beaten path, lovely weather, lovely scenery. It's a perfect location. But where are the 1800's era mansions? "What do you mean renovated!!" Mary McLaglen says inside her head. Outwardly, she smiles benignly and asks, "Are there any photographs of one before it was renovated? We'll have to build one for the movie set. And can we hurry, we have only six weeks before we're supposed to start shooting."

Mary will have some quiet times in a year, but none of them are between the first call from the studio saying they have a movie project and the wrap party, when the movie finishes shooting.

Mary McLaglen, a third generation movie maker, understands this business like few other people. When someone out there decides on a script, a director, and a cast, she gets this kind of call and starts her job: defining the budget, the schedule, the personnel, and the location, and most of all solving the kind of problems she faces here. "We need an 1800's mansion… Can we find one that needs restoration, and the owners are willing to exchange us using the house for three months for us doing the restoring for them!" What else will happen?

And once shooting starts, there will be other problems: weather, people who don't get along with each other, changes in nationality of characters that require the Brazilian actors to speak perfect Italian instead of Portuguese, and every other imaginable and unimaginable problem to troubleshoot.

Mary's job as Line Producer is to make sure the director has everyone and everything she (or he) needs to make the movie as originally envisioned, and for the amount of money and the amount of time she said it would.

But how did Mary McLaglen get here? Why is she doing this? Let her tell us her story, the story that parallels the history of the movie business in Hollywood.

4

Movie Business in Hollywood

I was born in Los Angeles, but I grew up nearly everywhere. My grandfather was an actor who won an academy award in 1935 and my father was a director, so it was almost preordained that my brother and I would work in the film business.

My father traveled a great deal, and my brother and I got to go with him! In those days, when my father did a lot of westerns with John Wayne, they would shoot several films in the same location, one after the other. So for instance, my tenth birthday was spent in Durango, Mexico.

I remember the villages, the tortillas and quesadillas, the tutors who tried to educate us from books, the strange wonderful world of new people and places which taught us more than the tutors, and the opportunities to actually work in the film industry at that age.

I was variously an extra, a makeup lady, an archaeologist, and a diplomat. I remember films shot in Mexico, South Africa, Ireland, England, Israel, and India… I'm sure I'm leaving something out.

It was a little more organized than that. As a child, I was an extra or just hung out, and of course searched for artifacts and visited with the local people. A film would take from four to six months, so the film crew would become my extended family.

When I was 18 and traveled with my father to South Africa, I was put to work in the makeup department and spent my days applying sweat and blood to the faces of hundreds of extras. I felt that I had a purpose; I was needed and therefore I felt fulfilled.

When I returned to the United States and the real world, I knew I needed to "make it on my own." My father says he knew I had already picked out my career path when I insisted on negotiating my own salary, instead of having him do it for me.

7

I asked a producer friend of our family's if I could have a job as a production coordinator. Since then, I have never stopped working.

My titles have changed from Production Coordinator, to Production Manager, to Co-Producer, and Executive Producer, but the responsibilities are very similar. I make decisions and I make things happen.

There were skills I had to learn on the job: making schedules and budgets using "Movie Magic"; how to anticipate what happens next; and problem solving.

But the most important skill is communication. Things can go terribly wrong if information isn't communicated properly. Getting along well with others is also very important. I learned from my mother who taught me empathy, and my father who taught me to find joy and goodness in everyday situations.

My job starts when the studio person hands me a script and asks me how much it will cost and how long it will take to shoot. I read the script and break down all the different scenes, different locations and cast members, while determining how complicated the scenes are, so I can figure out how much time we need to shoot it and how much it will cost.

The director and I hire the crew. I make sure everything is there for the director when we start to work, from the 1800s house we had renovated in Hot Springs, VA, for *Sommersby* to the lovely places in *Hope Floats* and *The Divine Secrets of the YaYa Sisterhood.*

I make sure that everything is on the set, from the caterers, to the costumes, to the makeup people. The lights and cameras are there and ready, and even sheets of paper for everyone telling them the scene and schedule for the next two days.

All the little details.

And although there is a lot more to do on a movie, my job usually ends when we finish shooting.

Post-production takes another six months, so that is handed over to the post-production supervisor. And then I rest a few weeks until I get the call to start on my next project.

At a very different time and place, a young woman hauling a 20-pound tape recorder and a long shotgun microphone tries to keep up with her partner, the cameraman/director, as he runs with his camera after several black French men dressed in colorful Mardi Gras costumes. The men are chasing a chicken around a barnyard, trying to catch it for a big gumbo that night. It is 1972 in Cajun country in southwest Louisiana, and Maureen Gosling, 22, is working on her first film, a documentary called *Dry Wood and Hot Pepper*. It's the first day she's ever used a tape recorder and it's a challenging initiation into the world of filmmaking.

During the next years, she learns a lot about sound recording while working on documentaries about a rock musician in Oklahoma, garlic lovers in Berkeley, and celebrations in New Orleans.

Burden of Dreams was shot in the Amazon rain forest about ten years later. This was a 16mm film documenting the making of a feature film about an Irishman who wanted to bring opera to the jungle. Maureen and the small documentary crew ran around filming a famous German director and his crew of 40 people, as they tried, among other things, to film a real 200-ton steamship being pulled over a mountain.

This documentary went on to achieve great success at film festivals and screenings around the world and Maureen went to places she never dreamed of going, like the Cannes Film Festival.

After 20 years and 20 films with director and filmmaker Les Blank, Maureen got to direct and produce her own film: *Blossoms of Fire,* about the women of Juchitán, Oaxaca, Mexico.

How did Maureen Gosling find herself in this strange and difficult world? How did she learn to excel as sound recordist, assistant editor, assistant cameraperson, editor, director, producer, and distributor? In short, how did she become an independent filmmaker? And most important of all, why did she want to be one?

Let her tell you her story: the story of a four-year old who wanted to grow up to be a circus lady; an eight-year old who wanted to grow up to be a missionary; a twelve-year old who wanted to be an artist; and a sixteen-year old who wanted to be a journalist – and became all those things as an independent filmmaker.

I was born in Colorado Springs, Colorado. My mother was Norwegian-Canadian. Although she didn't speak Norwegian, she taught my brother and sisters and me some of the Christmas traditions and had Norwegian knick-knacks in our house. I think it gave me my first interest in other cultures. My father was an army doctor, so, as many of you know, that means we moved several times and I grew up in several different worlds. The one that most affected me was Harlan, a small town in Kentucky where I went to elementary school. It was a town of 4,000 people in the Appalachian Mountains, where I witnessed poverty and segregation for the first time.

My father worked in a rehabilitation hospital, helping miners and other mountain people. Some of my classmates were very poor and I remember caring a lot about what they had to deal with in their everyday lives. I realized I was interested in people and their lives.

After four years, we moved. This time to Toledo, OH, where we stayed. My parents still live there.

Our family was very artistic. My father, in addition to being a doctor, was a jazz pianist and my mother loved working at a community theatre, sometimes as an actor. I went to lots of plays, I took piano lessons, and I loved to draw.

These activities helped me see how much I loved to express myself creatively and how attracted I was to the entertainment world.

But that didn't make it any easier to decide what I wanted to be when I grew up. In my brand new school in the big city of Toledo, I also focused on my English classes and worked on the school paper. I loved writing poems and stories, so at this time I thought I would be a journalist. But then one summer I volunteered at an inner city community center, which was very rewarding, so when I went to college, I chose the University of Michigan because it had a good school of Social Work. After a couple of years, I changed my mind and majored in Social Anthropology to learn about people in different cultures and customs.

At the university I also started watching lots and lots of foreign films. I got excited when I realized you could make films about different people and their cultures. So when I attended an Anthropological Film Festival that featured documentaries about people all over the world and their lives, I became enchanted with the power of film to connect me with those people. I felt that I learned more about different cultures in four days of watching films than I learned in two years of reading books.

At the same Anthropological Film Festival, I met Les Blank, an independent documentary filmmaker. He made films about people on the margins of American society. He focused especially on their music and the power of their cultural celebrations to help them transcend the difficulties of their lives.

Back home, I sent Les Blank a review I found of his films, and he started to write to me. I was thrilled to receive letters from a famous filmmaker. When I graduated, I didn't know what I was going to do next; then I saw Les at an Anthropology Conference. I mentioned to him that if he ever needed an assistant to please let me know. A couple of months later, he offered me a job and suddenly I was his apprentice, learning how to be a documentary filmmaker!

In this new role, the first film I worked on was *Dry Wood and Hot Pepper*. It was about the music and culture of the black French people of southwest Louisiana.

What was the first thing I learned as an apprentice? To be a sound recordist and a camera assistant. On my very first day, I recorded sound from 6:00 A.M. until about 2:00 A.M. the next morning, as we filmed people celebrating Mardi Gras Day and finishing at night with a big dance. I had to say "No" over and over to men who asked me to dance. It was the first time they'd seen a woman operating film equipment and they couldn't believe I was working rather than dancing.

I was worried about making mistakes, and I did make some. But with practice I got better and better. I would hold the microphone on a boom, being very still and quiet, getting everyone else to be quiet so I could get good sound, while Les was running the camera. As a camera assistant, I also had to learn to change the film, carefully taking out the film that Les had shot and putting in a fresh unexposed roll.

We were there for three months, so we had time to get to know people. I felt a lot of attachment to the people we filmed. One of the things I love most about my work is the opportunity to enter the worlds of people I never would have encountered working in an office. Films have taken me to Polish-American polka dances in the Midwest, to colorful fiestas in Mexico, to a Native American powwow in Oklahoma, to a Serbian-American wedding in Chicago, to a Buddhist temple in Kyoto, Japan.

After several years, I learned editing. Les taught me certain techniques and I also learned by watching him work. I studied how other films were cut. Soon I was able to edit films on my own.

Burden of Dreams was the most famous film I worked on, a documentary about the making of a feature film. It was my first experience on a dramatic film set.

It was also my first experience living in the Amazon rain forest far away from any city. There we lived in a beautiful jungle camp with the Brazilian, German, Peruvian, and indigenous cast members and crew of the feature film, the German director, and two magnificent steamships. I did sound recording and Les did camera work and we now had a third person, an assistant camera person who was also a translator and spoke Spanish, Portuguese, and German.

It was exciting to be with the native people, who wore red-orange face paint and handmade *cushmas* (their clothing), shot bows and arrows, and cooked meals over open fires. And it was thrilling and scary to film on board a steamship while it crashed through the most dangerous rapids in Peru.

This was the first film I edited all by myself. It took nine months. We premiered the film at the Cannes Film Festival and it went on to screen all over the world. It was enthusiastically received everywhere! To this day, I still meet people who know and like our documentary more than the feature film that we made it about!

For the last ten years, I've been working on my own film, *Blossoms of Fire,* as a director and producer.

And in yet another time and place, in a lovely suburban house in Hollywood, two 10-year-old girls are coming home from school. One of them calls out “Mom, I’ve got company!” and leads her friend into her mother’s office.

“My friend has some scary ideas about the movie business and I thought you could help me explain it to her.”

The young friend counts on her fingers: the film industry doesn’t care about women, black people, serious issues, or much of anything other than money…

Paula Weinstein, who has spent two decades working with virtually every major studio in the film industry, has to take a deep breath before attempting to enlighten this young girl. Paula’s titles have included senior vice-president and executive producer and she has not only enjoyed a powerful career herself, but she has worked with women from Jane Fonda and Barbara Streisand in films such as *Nine-to-Five* and *Yentl,* to Julia Roberts in *Something to Talk About.* These films, as well as many others that Paula has worked on, have helped to articulate women’s issues around workplace inequities, lack of equal educational opportunities, and social mores that treat women and minorities different from white men.

Her personal passion for politics led her to such projects as *Citizen Cohn* starring James Woods as the notorious McCarthy-era lawyer, and *Truman,* starring Gary Sinese as President Harry Truman.

And she was the official representative from the Hollywood film community when Nelson Mandela made his first official visit to the United States. She was lauded by organizations from the National Urban League to Women in Film. Maybe you could conclude that nobody else in Hollywood ever did anything, so they had to honor Paula, but she knew that she was only one of many who cared about a lot of things besides money.

She gently tried to explain all of this, and in reminiscing was reminded of the wonderful experiences she has had working with creative directors, actors, and producers to do the work she loves.

How did Paula Weinstein, a political activist involved in social issues, wind up as an honored producer with films and TV movies that have won many Academy Awards and Emmys? And most important of all, why did she want to be one?

Let her tell you her story: the story of a dedicated political activist, mother, and entertainment mogul.

PAULA WEINSTEIN
PAULA WEINSTEIN
PRODUCER

I was born in New York, but my two sisters and I grew up in England. My mother was a television producer and later a studio head who produced over 400 television programs in England.

I was sure of one thing in those days! I was never going to be a producer! It was too much work and too much of a struggle!

And in some strange twist of fate, both my sister, Lisa, and I are movie producers!!

We returned to the United States, New York to be exact, in 1963. My mother ran a studio in New York and continued to produce films and television programs. And somehow, I started my career as an assistant film editor in New York City.

I did take an assignment as Special Events Director in the office of Mayor John Lindsay, where I brought plays, ballets, and street festivals to the city's various communities.

At this time, I met Jane Fonda, who was involved in political activities that I found compelling. When she implied that I might be able to work on her projects, I relocated to Los Angeles and worked as a talent agent for International Creative Management (ICM) and later for William Morris.

Over the next 20 years, I worked in many positions involving production for various studios in Hollywood. From Vice President of Production at Warner Brothers to President of the Motion Picture Division at United Artists, to founder of two independent production companies, I have had the opportunity to do it all. Many of the feature films I helped develop, such as *The Fabulous Baker Boys* and *A Dry White Season,* have been nominated for Motion Picture Academy Awards. Many of my films, such as *Nine to Five* and *Something to Talk About,* have helped raise awareness of women's issues. Several of my TV movies, such as *Citizen Cohn* and *Truman,* brought home to viewers of the 90's some political realities of the 40's and 50's, while also winning Emmy nominations and awards, CableAce awards, and Golden Globe nominations.

At Spring Creek Productions, started in 1990 by Mark Rosenberg and me, my projects have included *Analyze This, Analyze That, The Perfect Storm, The Looney Tunes: Back In Action,* and *Envy.*

Movie making is done in three different phases with different people at work during the different phases: pre-production, production (the shoot), and post-production.

During pre-production the film or documentary is created. A script is written, the cast is selected, and a director is brought on board. After this part, which can take a long time, months or sometimes years, a producer will work from the script with the director and cast, to smooth out the details such as locations, schedules, set design, and costume design.

Mary
McLaglen

Production is an intense time of twelve-hour days, careful scheduling, troubleshooting, and anticipating problems. Whether we're dealing with a low-budget independent film or an amply-budgeted blockbuster, people have to have time to set up the sets, the lights, the sound recording equipment, and put out call sheets for the cast. Costumes appear magically, and makeup artists and hair technicians do their jobs early so that when cameras are starting to roll, the cast is starting to act and the director has everything she needs.

And for heaven's sake don't forget to feed everybody. The caterer may be the most important person after a long, hot day in the sun.

Maureen Gosling

I would hold the microphone on a boom!

Post-production seems like a relatively quiet time. The editors, sound mixers, graphics artists, and illustrators do a lot of their work alone as well as with the director.

But unfortunately, especially when deadlines are near, or if shooting took longer than expected, the post-production people are in for long hours and a lot of stress. The process starts out tediously, moves to incredibly creative, and ends up technical. Whether the process involves looking for tiny pieces of missing film, trying to get the DV Deck to talk to the computer, or converting procedures from one system to a newer one depends on which media you are using: film, digital-video, or video.

But in the end, the joy of turning the awful rough cut into a beautiful whole work of art happens on schedule. And then the marketers and publicists take over, but this book isn't about them.

Mary McLaglen tells us what a day is like for her as a line producer:

I'll get a call from the studio. They have a project for me! Usually they have a script, actor, and director. I first have to come up with an idea of what it will cost. I study the script for scenes and locations, and approximately how many shooting days will be required.

Of course I consult with the director on what she (or he) might be visualizing. I hire the production designer and the director of photography, and together we try to work out all the details. And I have about 12 weeks to get all of this done, so we can actually be ready to start shooting on schedule.

Let's say we just started shooting. Every night I try to anticipate possible problems and avert them. Every morning when I get to the set, I have breakfast and then have to deal with all the problems that I never anticipated. Everybody knows it never rains in California except the day we schedule an outdoor shoot and have to deal not only with rain but mud, which isn't in the script.

When the movie completes shooting, my job ends, and I hand it off to the post-production team, unwind, and go onto my next project.

What I like best about my job is that I am able to work with fascinating people. I've worked on a number of movies with Sandra Bullock, from *Hope Floats* to *Two Weeks Notice*. She's very talented and is loyal to the people she works with. I've gotten to work with people as both actors and directors, such as Forest Whittaker and Kiefer Sutherland. I particularly enjoy working in places I wouldn't ordinarily see, such as coal mines or prisons. I've learned more doing my job than I ever learned at school.

What I like least about my job is the incredible stress level. I feel the pressure to make sure that everything works.

I have to settle the conflicts between people, I have to fix the problems that arise, and worst of all, if someone isn't doing the job we need them to do, I have to let them go. With only a few hours to shoot each scene, we can't let someone learn on the job.

I feel a huge sense of achievement when the movie wraps. I've put months of my life into this film and I feel gratified to see it to completion. And I feel that way every time!

My future goals may make you laugh. I want to get married and have children. I've been so busy that it hasn't happened for me yet, and I don't want to put it off so far into the future that it will be too late!

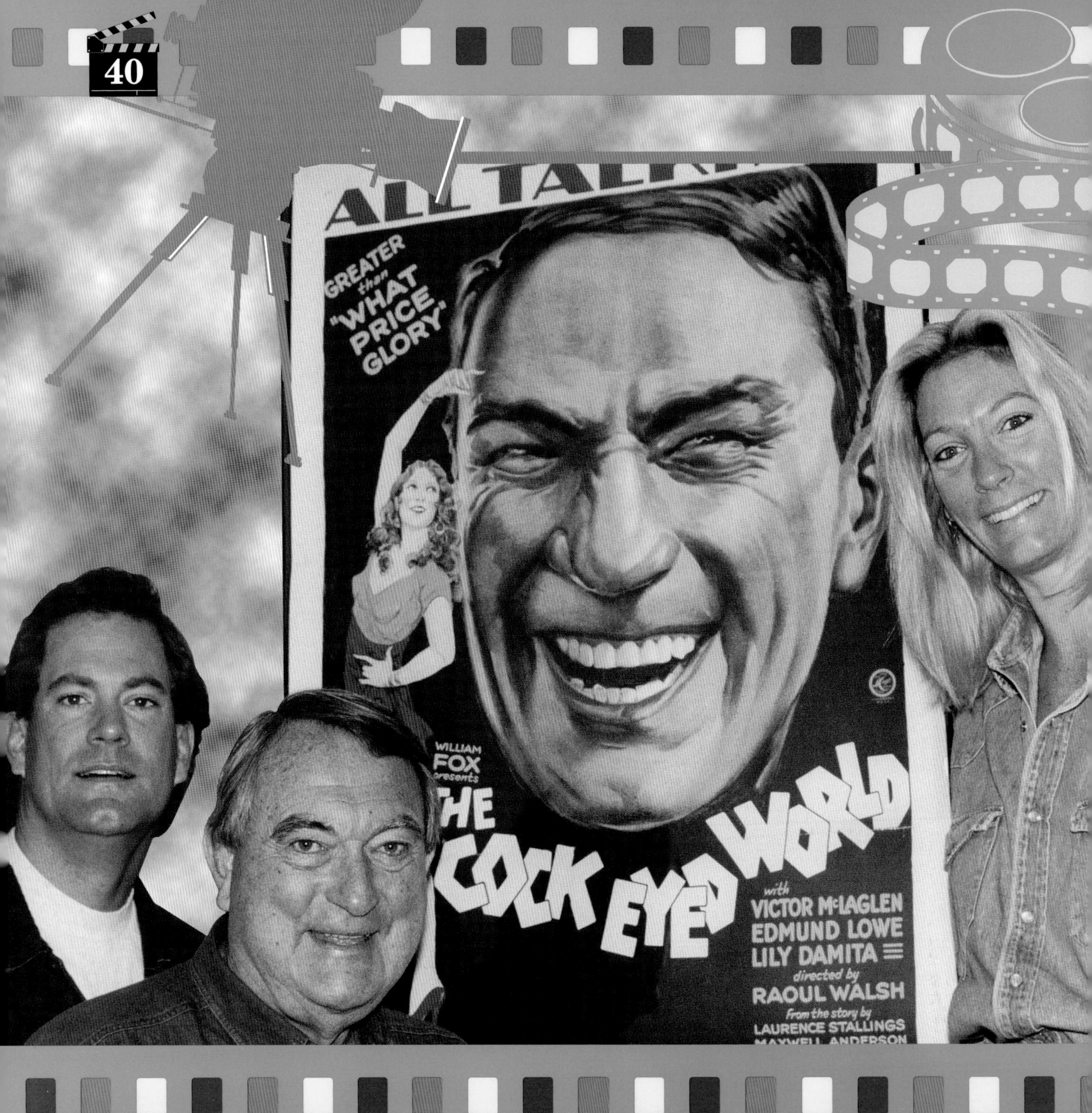
ALL TALK
GREATER than "WHAT PRICE GLORY"
WILLIAM FOX presents
THE COCK EYED WORLD
with
VICTOR McLAGLEN
EDMUND LOWE
LILY DAMITA
directed by
RAOUL WALSH
From the story by
LAURENCE STALLINGS

Maureen Gosling tells us what a day is like as an independent filmmaker:

For the last ten years, I've been working on my own film, *Blossoms of Fire,* as director and producer. *Blossoms of Fire* tells the story of a community in Mexico where the women are very important as breadwinners, as mothers, as organizers of local fiestas, and as teachers of the culture. They wear beautiful dresses covered with hand-embroidered flowers.

Before starting a film like this, I have to have a story that gets me excited, something I want to tell that hasn't been told before. As a documentary filmmaker, I want to share a vision, something people may not already know about. To realize that vision takes a lot of research, preparation, and imagination.

It also takes a lot of work to raise the money to pay for the many expenses of production and post-production. This can take a long time. For *Blossoms of Fire,* it took two years before we were even able to go to Mexico and shoot for six weeks.

Blossoms of Fire was my first chance to really direct. During the shoot, my partner, Ellen, and I had to plan before each day what we were going to shoot and when. We had to socialize with people to put them at ease about our filming and make sure we understood the local customs.

We had to communicate clearly with our crew about what we wanted them to do and make sure they had enough film and recording tape. Sometimes we had to have an alternative plan for the day, in case the weather wasn't good or someone didn't show up. We were also always watching out for what Les Blank calls "golden moments," unexpected things to shoot that we hadn't even thought of before.

After we finished shooting the film came post-production. That included editing and doing all the technical things required to make a clean and beautiful final product.

Post-production also included having to raise a lot of money. That was the biggest job I had as a producer on *Blossoms of Fire*. Because it took so long to acquire the funding we needed, I did editing jobs for other people to support myself, so the funds we generated could all go toward the film expenses.

Blossoms of Fire

The film wasn't done when it was done. The next step was to find a way to distribute it and market it so it could get out there and be seen. For most of the films I have worked on, the first step is showing the film at festivals, seeing if it has potential in theatres and television in the U.S. and abroad, and then marketing it to educational institutions and individuals.

I go to some of the film festivals, and often am invited to speak at screenings of the film at colleges or community groups. I talk about the people we filmed or about the filmmaking process. I love to hear and see people's reactions to my film, and the chances I have to interact with other filmmakers.

Although I have mostly worked on cultural and social issue documentaries, there are many, many kinds of documentaries to make. There are personal documentaries, documentaries about animals, biographies, historical documentaries, training documentaries, experimental documentaries, and much more!

What I like best about my work is that it's very creative,I often have flexible hours, travel, and meet interesting people. It is satisfying to watch the film with an audience and see them laugh or even cry.

What I like the least about my job are the technical problems. These include machines, such as camera and audio equipment, that break down and scheduling that creates the need to work really late sometimes. And of course, constant fund-raising.

My future goal is to make more of my own films. I have enough ideas to keep busy for many years! I look forward to seeing what life has in store and what I will do next.

Paula Weinstein tells us what a day is like as an executive producer:

My projects start when I get a script that will attract a director. Of course, if I loved the story, I've been working with writers to get the script in shape to attract a director and a studio.

I'm doing a lot of things simultaneously: making deals with various participants: director, cinematographer, and actors; and working with the director to scout locations and collect a crew; and negotiating a budget that fits the people, places, and concepts that my movie will require.

And finally, we're ready with the locations, the sets, the costumes, and the crew. We can start shooting.

During the shooting, I go to the set before the "crew call" and work with the director. I discover the production problems that need to be dealt with and most important to me, I get to see, creatively, what my movie is becoming.

After shooting is complete and during post-production, the director and the editor will work for about 8 to 10 weeks to create a "first cut." When it's ready, we show it to the studio.

And I even am involved in the marketing decisions, like what will be in the trailer or the ads.

Because the process can take a long time, sometimes I'm working on multiple projects: looking at the script for my next movie, working on a current movie and dealing with marketing my previous movie.

Paula
Weinstein

What I like best about my work is putting a project together. I like falling in love with a story and wanting to see it told! And sometimes that can take a long time and many steps.

I love being in the editing room with a director and seeing the story I imagined come alive.

What I like the least about my work is the fighting! I may have the story I love and a good script to tell that story, but the studio doesn't see it or none of the actors or directors that I want is interested in the project. It takes a lot of passion and tenacity to keep up the fight until someone finally sees what I see, or is just too exhausted to argue me out of it anymore!

Another thing I like least about being the producer is that while I know how much I do to make a movie what it is, very often the credit (or the blame) goes to the director, and I'm invisible and anonymous! Oh well.

Lots of Passion
To Get It Done!

How can you tell if you would be good at movie making? First of all consider the following about movie making:

During the pre-production phases, diverse talents are required, from script writing to set and costume design, and from location scouting to raising money. During the production phase the diverse talents involve creative skills such as set construction, makeup, acting and directing, technical skills such as lighting and operating electronic equipment, and administrative skills such as scheduling and budgeting.

During the post-production phases the diverse skills run the gamut from marketing and packaging to editing and creating special effects. With such a varied set of talents, almost anyone can find something that they are capable of doing. But what qualities are uniquely required of movie makers that don't apply to novelists or electrical engineers?

Documentary Film Making

1. *Are you willing and able to work as part of a team? Do you enjoy interacting with people and getting them to work together?*

One person alone cannot create a movie. The diverse list of talents can require a group of 20 for a low budget independent film to a group of hundreds for a relatively moderate sized movie, so the movie maker needs to have the ability to communicate, motivate, and negotiate and compromise so the entire team can work together more efficiently, more comfortably, and ultimately, more successfully.

2. Can you visualize something that doesn't exist and see all the details in your head? Are you motivated to work long and hard to make that vision come alive?

The movie maker, like artists and architects, is dealing with something that does not yet exist in the real world, until the artist or movie maker finishes it.

Before the process can get started, the person with the "inner vision" has to sell it to funders, actors, and directors to get the movie made.

During the process, the person with the "inner vision" has to share that with the team who is to help build it, and so she needs to be able to experience, in all its colors and textures, what she sees and feels.

3. Are you able to focus on all of the details and solve all the day-to-day problems that may be encountered?

An engineering teacher once said: “The bridge either holds up or falls down. That’s when you know if you were right or wrong.” And the bridge holds up if all the designs were correct, the plans reflected the design, and the screws and bolts were put in the places the plan required.

A movie is at least as complicated as a bridge and all the details need to be dealt with according to the plans and designs.

4. Are you able to handle the stress?

Whether you're dealing with a huge blockbuster film and appropriate budget, or a small independent film that has a few concerned investors, a movie maker is using other people's money, lots of it, and dealing with schedules. When some of the many things that can go wrong do go wrong, will you be able to take a deep breath, smile, and get on with fixing the problems and creating the work of your lifetime? Do you have the tenacity and the strength of character it takes to keep going when no one else shares your vision?

To be a good movie maker, either in dramatic films or documentaries, it is necessary to have some experience performing the role of each person on a film team. This will help you to be aware of each person's role and give you an appreciation of each person's needs in the production.

For example:

If you have worked as a sound recordist, you know how long it takes to set up microphones and tape players – something that every director must know.

If you have worked as an editor, you know that enough different images must be shot to create a well rounded story – something every cameraperson must know.

If you have been a cameraperson, you know how the camera picks up light and what makes a good image in the frame – something every lighting technician must know.

To Be A Good Movie Maker

To become a movie maker:

1. Learn by doing: make a film on your own with a video camera and learn how to use equipment.
2. Observe carefully a lot of good movies and read books about them.
3. Apprentice with a movie maker whose work you like.
4. Go to film school. Be a producing fellow at a film school.
5. Fall in love with a story or have a vision you would like to share with the world. This will motivate you to figure out a way to get it out there.

As a movie maker you can work on independent productions; you can do commercial work; you can do freelance work; you can work for a film festival, a television station, or a production company.

You can do it too! You can be a woman movie maker.

YOU CAN BE A WOMAN MOVIE MAKER

MOVIE MAKER LESSON PLAN 1

PURPOSE: To gain an understanding of how a film goes from a paper script to a production.

MATERIALS: Copy of a few pages from a play, glue, scissors, marker pens, construction paper, cardboard, and masking tape.

PROCEDURES: Have the children read the play aloud and decide what movements the characters will have (e.g., picking up a spoon, answering the telephone).
Have them make a list of what different shots will be required to capture the action of the scene. Assign each child one or two shot drawings to make. Have them draw the action, using as much perspective as they can. Cut out the drawings and mount on construction paper.
Have the children arrange the individual shots as a story board (like a comic strip, in sequence). The storyboard translates the story into pictures.

CONCLUSIONS: What did you choose to put into the storyboard that wasn't in the words? Why?

MOVIE MAKER LESSON PLAN 2

PURPOSE: To understand lighting and shadows.

MATERIALS: Flashlight, colored gels, white poster board.

PROCEDURES: Have children form pairs. One child gets a flashlight, and shines it on the right side of the other child's face, then the left side, then, underneath, then above, then from faraway, and from short distances. Have the children reverse and the other child does the same.
If the room has natural light and windows, open any blinds or drapes,

and then close them. If possible, place one child in partial sunlight next to a window.
Using flashlights or lamps or sunlight, have one child hold up gels in front of the light, or bounce the light off white poster board onto the other child. Have the children make notes on how they look, what kind of shadows they see.

CONCLUSIONS: What did you find when you used the gels? Did you prefer the lights on or off?

MOVIE MAKER LESSON PLAN 3

PURPOSE: Develop an understanding of how the camera helps to tell a story.

MATERIALS: TV set, paper, marker pens, poster board, watch with second hand.

PROCEDURES: Have the class watch a TV show with the sound turned off.
Have them time the length of the shots, and observe the different kinds of shots: close-ups, panning shots, etc. (refer to the Glossary for the names of different kinds of shots.)
Have each child draw one of the children from a different angle and distance. Place several of these on the poster board in successive pictures. Have one child make up a story about the pictures.
Jumble the pictures and select a different set in a different order.
Have another child make up a story about these pictures.

CONCLUSIONS: How does the angle of the camera or the distance influence what you see? How much does the camera move in a scene of only a few minutes?

MOVIE MAKER LESSON PLAN 4

PURPOSE: Practice designing sets and costumes.

MATERIALS: Color photographs of subject, cardboard boxes such as shoe boxes, markers, fabrics, pens, popsicle sticks, cardboard rolls.

PROCEDURES: Have the children divide into groups of five or six to a shoebox. Have them first decide on an overall plan: three college classrooms, and then assign each group to one particular "set." One child can do the room interior, one the exterior, one the furniture. Be aware of the use of color to convey the mood, motifs such as church steeples, or plaid clothing.

CONCLUSIONS: How do you convey a particular time and place? What motifs did you use to give people clues as to what they were looking at?

MOVIE MAKER LESSON PLAN 5

PURPOSE: Practice acting and directing.

MATERIALS: Several copies of a scene from a play, pens, paper.

PROCEDURES: Choose a director and a casting director. Have the casting director choose classmates to play different parts.
Have the director work with the actors, rehearse them, and help them to visualize the part.
Do the scene.
Choose a different director, casting director and cast members.
Repeat the work and the scene.
Have the class discuss the different jobs of director, casting director, and cast, and how they saw the interaction.

CONCLUSIONS: Was the scene done the same both times? How did it differ, and why did it happen?
Does the class have recommendations to casting directors and directors?

MOVIE MAKER LESSON PLAN 6

PURPOSE: To put all the previous pieces together and learn to produce a film.

MATERIALS: Script of scene, storyboard of scene, costumes, set (decorated classroom), video camera, recordable video tape.

PROCEDURES: Choose a producer who will assign everyone else their jobs: director, actors, cameraperson, crew. Allow everyone to confer: director with actors and cameraperson, producer with everyone, etc.
Set up, rehearse, and then videotape the scene.

CONCLUSIONS: What kind of production problems were encountered?
After viewing the scene what suggestions for change could be made?

MOVIE MAKER LESSON PLAN 7

PURPOSE: To learn how messages are gotten across in the media.

MATERIALS: Television, note pad, pens.

PROCEDURES: Observe television for a certain time (one hour, one evening, network or educational). Tabulate the number of times you see stories that include: men/women; people of different ethnicities, ages, abilities/disabilities; body types; professions.

CONCLUSIONS: Do you see your own face on television? Whose faces do you see?

MOVIE MAKER LESSON PLAN 8

PURPOSE: Learn about documentaries.

MATERIALS: Note-pad, pens, camera or tape recorder.

PROCEDURES: Pick someone in your life whom you find particularly interesting.
Make a list of 5-10 questions you would like to ask them that would encourage them to tell you about themselves (not yes or no questions)
Ask them if you could do a taped or videotaped interview with them.
Document an hour in the life of a classmate, friend, or teacher.
Think about how a setting can express something about the person or their story.
Discuss with said person what activities they would like documented, and decide who else they might be interacting with: their home, their place of work, their favorite place, photographs, and after making notes, film the activities and dialogues and perhaps interview other people who can tell you more about them.

Glossary

2-shot: a shot where two subjects are on the screen
art director: person in charge of bring to life the production designer's vision, in charge of set building, props
barn doors: hinged flaps on a light that direct where the light flows
boom: a pole for the microphone that can be hung above or below the actors to pick up dialogue but not be picked up visually in the camera
close-up: a shot where the subject fills up most of the frame, if shooting a person then it is their head and shoulders
color spectrum: realm of color from violet to red
color correction: a post production term for cleaning up master tapes to correct skin tones predominately
costume designer: person in charge of creating the wardrobe
cutaway: a shot in a scene of something other than the main dialogue or action
director: the person that is in charge of creating the overall visual aesthetic of the film, sets, actors, costumes, camera shots.
director of photography or cinematographer: person responsible for the look of the photography, in charge of the camera and lighting crews
diffuse light: soft light like from a common light bulb
dolly shot: a shot where the camera moves on a vehicle called a dolly
dub: copying of a tape, AKA dupe for duplication
egg crate: a metal frame added to soft light sources to make them more directional
extreme close-up: a shot where the screen is filled with just the subject's face
foley: creating and recording sound effects while the film is played, done on a sound stage using props, named after Jack Foley who started the technique
flats: large wooden structures used to make the walls of the set
flag: a black cloth used to block light
fade out: a process done in editing where the scene dissolves into black
globes: professional term for light bulbs

grips: persons on the set in charge of setting up lights and erecting sets
hard light: direct, focused light
lavalier: a small, clip-on mic
line producer: person in charge of keeping on schedule form scene to scene
medium shot: a shot where the subject and some background are on the screen, if shooting a person it is from their waist up
over-the-shoulder: a shot of a person from over the shoulder of the person they are having dialogue with
pan: movement of the camera along a horizontal plane
pedestal: a vertical pan from a person's feet to their head
point-of-view: a shot done from the perspective of the subject
producer: the person in charge of book keeping, scheduling, problem solving, coordinating
production designer: the person in charge of designing the sets and props
reverse: the opposite perspective in an over the shoulder shot
stingers: extension chords
sides: a dialogue only version of a script making readings easier for the actors
slating: when recording audio separately for the film, the process of holding a slate which has the scene number and take written on it, the clapper on the slate can be used to sync the sound
sync: the process of synchronizing the sound with the visual
slow motion: a shot that plays at a slower speed
slow reveal: often a pan or dolly shot that reveals the scene slowly
shotgun: a mic that is often attached to a camera or a boom
soft light: diffuse light, a lower wattage bulb
three-point lighting: a standard way of lighting a subject using a strong directed key light, a soft fill light, and a strong back light
wattage: the amount of electrical power that a light uses defines its intensity
wide shot: a shot that captures all of the subject's body as well as much of the scenery
wipe: a type of transition where one image is wiped over the next
zoom: a process of transitioning from a wide shot to a close-up

About the Authors:

Mary McLaglen, Producer.
Mary McLaglen has been credited as Producer on a dozen major motion pictures. Having grown up in the film industry, Mary started working in films as a child extra and worked her way up through various backstage positions such as makeup and production coordination. She has participated in filmmaking for more than 30 years, but 10 years ago, on *Sommersby,* she was entrusted with Producer responsibility. Ms. McLaglen has worked as Co-Producer, Production Manager, or Producer on *Last Light, The Client, Moonlight & Valentino, Sgt. Bilko, One Fine Day, Hope Floats, Practical Magic, Pay it Forward, The Divine Secrets of the YaYa Sisterhood, Two Weeks Notice,* and *Envy.* Mary is a member of the Director's Guild and the Producer's Guild. She resides both in Los Angeles, CA, and Friday Harbor, WA.

Maureen Gosling, Producer, Director, Editor.
Although best known for her twenty-year collaboration with acclaimed independent director, Les Blank, Gosling has participated in all aspects of documentary filmmaking for more than 30 years. She was co-filmmaker, editor and/or sound recordist with Blank on 20 16mm films they made together, including *J'ai été au Bal: The Cajun,* and *Zydeco Music of Louisiana,* and *Burden of Dreams* (on the tribulations of German director Werner Herzog shooting his feature *Fitzcarraldo* in the Peruvian Amazon). Gosling has also been sought after as an editor by numerous directors, editing such films as *A Dream in Hanoi, Bomba: Dancing the Drum* and Shakti Butler's *The Way Home.* Her work often focuses on themes of people and their cultural values, music as cultural expression, and the changing gender roles of men and women. *Burden of Dreams,* Gosling and Blank's most internationally well-known film, received a British Academy Award in 1983 for Best Documentary Feature, and was on 12 U.S. Critics' Top Ten List of the Best Films. In 1982. Gosling was nominated for

Best Editing by the American Cinema Editors for *Burden of Dreams.* Her films have been seen in countless film festivals around the world, on national public and cable television, on television in Europe, Australia and Asia, and have been distributed widely to educational institutions. In recent years, Gosling has co-produced and directed her own independent documentary *Blossoms of Fire* celebrating the Isthmus Zapotec people of southern Oaxaca, Mexico.
For more information: http://www.maureengosling.com

Paula Weinstein, Producer.
Ms. Weinstein oversees Baltimore Spring Creek Productions with partner Barry Levinson, and has worked with virtually every major studio in the film industry. Beginning her career working as an assistant film editor in New York City, she became Special Events Director responsible for bringing entertainment to the city's small communities. Over 30 years ago, she moved to Los Angeles as a talent agent where her clients included Jane Fonda and Donald Sutherland. Paula developed and produced films such as *Nine to Five, Brubaker, Body Heat, War Games,* and *Yentl* as Vice President of Production for first Warner Brothers, then 20th Century Fox, then Ladd Company, and then United Artists. In 1984 Weinstein started WW Productions, an independent production company, and later Spring Creek Productions. Her independent projects, such as *A Dry White Season, The Fabulous Baker Boys, Fearless, Flesh and Bone, Analyze This, Analyze That, The Perfect Storm,* and *Looney Tunes: Back In Action,* received among them six academy award nominations.

Judith Love Cohen, author.
Cohen is a Registered Professional Electrical Engineer with bachelor's and master's degrees in engineering from the University of Southern California and University of California, Los Angeles. She has written plays, screenplays, and newspaper articles in addition to her series of children's books that began with *You Can Be a Woman Engineer.*

Acknowledgements:

Jerry Bishop and Maurice Hewitt for research and contributions on the technical aspects of movie making.
Photographs supplied by authors:
Mary McLaglen – family photographs pages 4, 7, 31, 40, 51 and front cover and back cover; Copyright Brian Hamill 2002, page 38
Paula Weinstein – photographs pages 25, 29, 48, 59 and front and back cover
Maureen Gosling – family photographs page 13; Copyright Chris Simon Page 43; Copyright Werner Herzog page 53; Copyright Les Blank pages 18, 33, 35, front cover, back cover; Copyright John Fago page 53
Judith L. Cohen – photos courtesy Bobi Jackson, Cascade Pass, Inc. front and back cover
The attached DVD contains interviews about the following movie maker's work and related film clips for some of them:
Mary McLaglen; Judith Love Cohen; Cameron Fuller; Marjorie Kaye; Bobi Jackson; and Kate Johnson interviews photographed by Frederic Humberic and edited by Fidel Gruber
Maureen Gosling provided *Maureen Gosling, Documentary Film Maker* interview photographed by Emiko Omori and edited by Maureen Gosling with short clips of *Always for Pleasure, Burden of Dreams, Dry Wood,* and *In Heaven There Is No Beer?* courtesy of Les Blank, Flower Films; *A Dream in Hanoi* courtesy of Tom Weidlinger, Moira Productions; *Blossoms of Fire* courtesy of New Yorker Films, Nadia Brunner-Velásquez, interviewer
Short films on the DVD include *How I Met Alex* by Cameron Fuller; *Beware of Dog* by Marjorie Kaye with music score courtesy of Jethro Jeremiah Demers; *Living Arts on the Road to Hawaii* by Bobi Jackson; *Between Thoughts* by Kate Johnson; *Count Down* and excerpts from *Future Girls: Adventures in Marine Biology* Copyright 2003 courtesy of Cascade Pass Productions by Judith Love Cohen; Music score composed and performed by Suzanne Weiss Morgen and Rachel Siegel (flute) and lyrics by David Katz and Suzanne Weiss Morgen.
DVD Graphics and animations and programming by David A. Katz and Fidel Gruber
Support for this project from Wells Fargo Private Client Services, International Documentary Association, New Moon Publications, Lightning Dubbs and QRS Software.

71

New Moon

The Magazine for Girls and Their Dreams

New Moon
Soul

Documentaries are fun and exciting
and can explore many different subjects.
At the International Documentary Association
we can help you learn
more about documentary films,
and how to make them.
Please visit us online at
www.documentary.org
IDA